PHOTO CREDITS

Gene Ahrens   49
Michael Blate/TOM STACK & ASSOC.   55
G. Mathew Brady/TOM STACK & ASSOC.   41
William R. Eastman/TOM STACK & ASSOC.   29
Berne Greene, cover
Mark Keller/TOM STACK & ASSOC.   37
William Koechling   53
Whitney L. Lane/TOM STACK & ASSOC.   47
Jay Lurie/TOM STACK & ASSOC.   11
Larry G. McKee   43
Peterson/PUBLIX PICTORIAL SERVICE   7
Paul Sharp   13, 17, 31
Tom Stack/TOM STACK & ASSOC.   35
Barbara Von Hoffmann/TOM STACK & ASSOC.   25
E. E. Webber   19
Herman Wohrstein   23

He is risen

THOMAS MERTON

ARGUS COMMUNICATIONS • NILES, IL 60648

International Standard Book
No.: 0-913592-58-7

Library of Congress Catalog Card
No.: 75-18973

    2 3 4 5 6 7 8 9

"He has risen,
he is not here . . .
he is going before you to Galilee."
(Mark 16:6-7)

Christ is risen. Christ lives.
Christ is the Lord
of the living and the dead.
He is the Lord of history.

Christ is the Lord
of a history that moves.
He not only holds
the beginning and the end
in his hands,
but he is in history with us,
walking ahead of us
to where we are going.
He is not always
in the same place.

The cult of the Holy Sepulchre
is Christian only in so far
as it is the cult
of the place
where Christ is no longer found.
But such a cult
can be valid
only on one condition:
that we are willing to move on,
to follow him
to where we are not yet,
to seek him
where he goes before us—
"to Galilee."

So we are called
not only to believe
that Christ once rose
from the dead,
thereby proving that
he was God;
we are called to
experience the Resurrection
in our own lives
by entering
into this dynamic movement,
by following Christ
who lives in us.
This life,
this dynamism,
is expressed
by the power of love
and of encounter:
Christ lives in us
if we love one another.
And our love
for one another means
involvement
in one another's history.

Christ lives in us
and leads us,
through mutual encounter
and commitment,
into a new future
which we build together
for one another.
That future is called
the Kingdom of God.
The Kingdom
is already established;
the Kingdom
is a present reality.
But there is still work to be done.
Christ calls us
to work together
in building his Kingdom.
We cooperate with him
in bringing it to perfection.

Such is the timeless message
of the Church
not only on Easter Sunday
but on every day
of the year
and every year
until the world's end.
The dynamism
of the Easter mystery
is at the heart
of the Christian faith.
It is the life of the Church.
The Resurrection
is not a doctrine
we try to prove
or a problem
we argue about:
it is the life
and action
of Christ himself
in us
by his Holy Spirit.

A Christian
bases his entire life
on these truths.
His entire life
is changed
by the presence
and the action
of the Risen Christ.

He knows
he has encountered
the Risen Christ,
as Paul encountered him
on the road to Damascus.
Such an encounter
does not have to be dramatic,
but it has to be
personal
and real.
Baptism is, of course,
the seal
and sign
of this encounter.

But Baptism
must be lived out
in subsequent encounters
with Christ:
in the Eucharist,
in the other sacraments,
in reading and hearing
the word of God,
and in realizing that
the word
is preached to us
personally.
True encounter with Christ
in the word of God
awakens something
in the depth of our being,
something
we did not know was there.

True encounter with Christ
liberates something in us,
a power
we did not know we had,
a hope,
a capacity for life,
a resilience,
an ability to bounce back
when we thought
we were completely defeated,
a capacity to grow
and change,
a power
of creative transformation.

For the Christian
there is no defeat,
because Christ is risen
and lives in us,
and Christ has overcome
all
that seeks to destroy us
or to block
our human
and spiritual growth.

In the Easter sequence
the Church sings
of the duel
of death and life in our heart.
This is a bitter,
desperate fight,
the combat of life and death
in us,
the battle of human despair
against Christian hope.

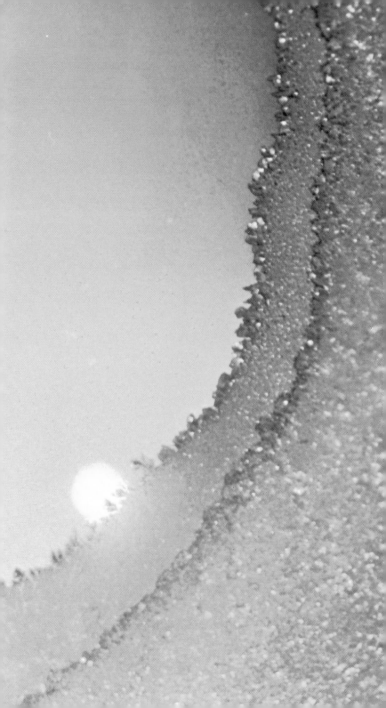

The risen life
is not easy;
it is also a dying life.
The presence
of the Resurrection
in our lives
means
the presence of the Cross,
for we do not
rise with Christ
unless we also first die
with him.
It is by the Cross
that we enter
the dynamism
of creative transformation,
the dynamism
of resurrection and renewal,
the dynamism
of love.

The teaching of St. Paul
is centered entirely
on the Resurrection.
How many Christians
really understand
what St. Paul is talking about
when he tells us
that we have
"died to the Law"
in order to rise
with Christ?
How many Christians
dare to believe
that he who is risen with Christ
enjoys the liberty
of the sons of God
and is not bound
by the restrictions
and taboos
of human prejudice?

To be risen
with Christ
means not only
that one has **a choice**
and that one **may** live
by a higher law—
the law of grace
and love—
but that one **must** do so.

The first obligation
of the Christian
is to maintain his freedom
from all superstitions,
all blind taboos
and religious formalities,
indeed from all
empty forms of legalism.

Read the Epistle to the Galatians
again some time.
Read it in light
of the Church's summons
to complete renewal.

The Christian
must have the courage
to follow Christ.
The Christian
who is risen in Christ
must dare
to be like Christ:
he must dare
to follow conscience
even in unpopular causes.
He must, if necessary,
be able to disagree with the majority
and make decisions
that he knows
to be according to the Gospel
and teaching of Christ,
even when others
do not understand
why he is acting this way.

We do not rise with Christ
unless we also first die with him.

"The followers of Christ
are called by God
not according to their accomplishments,
but according
to his own purpose
and grace."*
This statement
effectively disposes
of a Christian
inferiority complex
which makes people think
that because
they never have amounted to anything
in the eyes of others,
they can never
amount to anything
in the eyes of God.
Here again
we see another aspect
of St. Paul's teaching on freedom.

*Council Constitution on the Church, n. 40

24

Too many Christians
are not free
because they submit
to the domination
of other people's ideas.
They submit
passively
to the opinions of the crowd.
For self-protection
they hide in the crowd,
and run along
with the crowd—
even when it turns
into a lynch mob.
They are afraid of the
aloneness,
the moral nakedness,
which they would feel
apart from the crowd.

But the Christian
in whom Christ is risen
dares
to think and act differently
from the crowd.

He has ideas of his own,
not because he is arrogant,
but because
he has the humility to stand alone
and pay attention
to the purpose
and the grace of God,
which are often
quite contrary
to the purposes
and the plans
of an established
human power structure.

. . . to maintain freedom from
all empty forms of legalism.

If we have risen
with Christ
then we must dare
to stand by him
in the loneliness
of his Passion,
when the entire establishment,
both religious and civil,
turned against him
as a modern state
would turn against
a dangerous radical.
In fact,
there **were** "dangerous radicals"
among the Apostles.

The Christian must dare
to follow his conscience
even in unpopular causes.

Simon the Zealot
was a member
of the extreme left wing
of Jewish politics,
a would-be freedom fighter
against Roman imperial rule.

If we study the trial
and execution
of Jesus
we find that he was condemned
on the charge
that he was a revolutionary,
a subversive radical,
fighting for the overthrow
of legitimate government.

This was not true
in the political sense.
Jesus
stood entirely outside
of all Jewish politics,
because his Kingdom
was not of this world.
But his actions could be twisted
to look like
political revolutionism.
And yet he was
a ``freedom fighter''
in a different way.
His death
and resurrection
were the culminating battle
in his fight
to liberate us
from **all** forms of tyranny,
all forms of domination
by anything or anyone
except the Spirit,
the Law of Love,
the ``purpose and grace''
of God.

When we understand
these things,
we can understand
what lies behind St. Paul's words
in praise of the freedom
which comes
only in the Cross
and Resurrection
of Christ:
"When Christ freed us,"
said Paul,
"he meant us
to remain free.
Stand firm, therefore,
and do not submit again
to the yoke of slavery."

. . . the humility to stand alone
and pay attention to
the purpose and grace of God.

This is in the Epistle
to the Galatians (5:1),
where Paul rebukes
the Christian converts
for still thinking
that certain legal observances
were necessary for them:
as if
they could not be saved
without being circumcised.
The Galatian converts
were tempted to something
that we might describe today
as religious overkill.
They wanted
to make absolutely sure
that everything
was completely taken care of.

We must dare to stand by Christ
in the loneliness of his Passion.

So they not only adopted
the Christian faith
but all the ritual practices
of Judaism as well.
Thus, if Christianity
turned out to be
not good enough,
they would still be covered
by Jewish observance!

This spirit of overkill
is characteristic
of the Christian
who is afraid to be
simply a Christian
in the world of our time.
He is not content
with faith
in the Risen Christ,
not content
with the grace and love
of Christ:
he wants the comfort
and justification
of being on the side
of wealth and power.
In some cases,
Christianity
becomes literally
the religion of overkill:

the religion in which you prove
your fidelity to Christ
by your willingness
to destroy his enemies
ten times over.
In order to do this
you have to conveniently forget
all those disturbing statements
in the New Testament
about the love of enemies!

St. Paul says,
"The whole of the Law
is summarized
in a single command:
Love your neighbor as yourself. . . .
If you are guided
by the Spirit
you will be in no danger
of yielding to self-indulgence,
since self-indulgence is the opposite
of the Spirit."
(Galatians 5:14-16)
He goes on
to outline the hard line
of self-denial
which is inseparable
from the Cross of Christ.

We have been called
to share in the Resurrection
of Christ
not because
we have fulfilled all the laws
of God and man,
not because
we are religious heroes,
but because
we are suffering and struggling
human beings,
sinners
fighting for our lives,
prisoners
fighting for freedom,
rebels
taking up spiritual weapons
against the powers that degrade
and insult our human dignity.

42

If we had been able
to win the battle
for freedom
without his help,
Christ would not have come
to fight for us and with us.
But he has come
to gather us around him
in the battle
for freedom.
The fact
that we have been wounded
in the fight,
or the fact
that we may have spent
most of the time,
so far,
running away from the battle
makes no difference now.
He is with us.
He is risen.

———

The Gospel account
of the Resurrection
in Mark
is very suggestive.
Not only
is the Resurrection
the key
and center
of the Christian life,
but our Easter experience
often follows the pattern
of the experience
of the Apostles
and other witnesses
of the Resurrection.
The experience
of the holy women at the tomb
gives us a typical example
of the dynamics of Christian faith.

We have been called to share in the
Resurrection of Christ because we are
suffering and struggling human beings.

We often forget
that in all accounts
of the Resurrection,
the witnesses started out
with the unshakeable conviction
that Christ was dead.
The women
going to the tomb
thought of Jesus
as dead and gone.

They had only one thing
in mind:
to embalm his body.
But there was a problem.
The tomb was sealed
with a stone
too heavy
for them to move.
They did not know how
they would find someone
who would roll away
the stone
for them
so they could come
to his dead body.

Now this is a kind
of psychological pattern
for the way
we too often act
in our Christian lives.
Though we may
still "say" with our lips
that Christ is risen,
we secretly believe him,
in practice,
to be dead.
And we believe
that there is a massive stone
blocking the way
and keeping us
from getting to his dead body.
Our Christian religion
too often becomes
simply the cult
of the dead body of Christ
compounded with anguish
and desperation
over the problem
of moving the immovable stone
that keeps us
from reaching him.

48

This is no joke.
This is what actually happens
to the Christian religion
when it ceases to be
a really living faith
and becomes
a mere legalistic
and ritualistic formality.
Such Christianity
is no longer life
in the Risen Christ
but a formal cult
of the dead Christ
considered not as
the Light and Savior of the world
but as
a kind of divine "thing,"
an extremely holy object,
a theological relic.

This is the result
of substituting
something else
for the Living Presence
and Light of Christ
in our lives.
Instead of the unspeakable,
invisible,
yet terribly near and powerful
presence of the Living Lord,
we set up a structure
of pious images
and abstract concepts
until Christ becomes a shadow.
At last
he becomes
a corpse-like figure of wax.
Yet people go
to extraordinary lengths
to venerate this inert object,
to embalm it
with all kinds of perfumes,
and to make up fantastic tales
about what it can do
to make you rich
and happy
by its powerful magic.

We must never
let our religious ideas,
customs, rituals, and conventions
become more real to us
than the Risen Christ.
We must learn,
with St. Paul,
that all these religious accessories
are worthless
if they get in the way of
our faith
in Jesus Christ,
or prevent us
from loving our brother
in Christ.
Paul looked back
on the days
when he had been
a faultless observer
of religious law,
and confessed
that all this piety
was **meaningless.**
He rejected it as worthless.
He wanted one thing only.
Here are his words:

"I believe nothing can happen
that will outweigh
the supreme advantage
of knowing Christ Jesus
my Lord.
For him
I have accepted the loss of everything,
and I look on everything
as so much rubbish,
if only
I can have Christ
and be given a place
in him.
I am no longer
trying for perfection
by my own efforts . . .
but I want only the perfection
that comes from faith in Christ. . . .
All I want to know
is Christ
in the power of his Resurrection
and to share his sufferings
by reproducing
the pattern of his death."
(Philippians 3:8-11)

54

When the holy women
arrived at the tomb,
they found the stone
was rolled away.
But the fact
that the stone was rolled away
made little difference,
since the body of Jesus
was not there anyway.
The Lord had risen.
So too with us.
We create
obscure religious problems
for ourselves,
trying desperately to break through
to a dead Christ
behind a tombstone.
Such problems are absurd.
Even if we could
roll away the stone,
we would not find his body
because he is not dead.

He is not
an inert object,
not a lifeless thing,
not a piece of property,
not a super-religious heirloom:
HE IS NOT THERE,
HE IS RISEN.

The Christian life,
Christian worship,
Christian community,
the Eucharist,
all these
have been obscured
by a limited ritualistic piety
that insists
on treating the Risen Lord
as if he were a dead body,
a holy object,
not Spirit
and Life,
and Son of the Living God.

Today,
let us come with faith
to the banquet of the Lamb,
the Risen Savior,
to the Bread of Life
that is not the food
of the dead
but the true and Risen
Body of Christ.
He who encounters
the Risen Christ
in the banquet
of his Body and Blood
will live forever!

Come,
People of God,
Christ our Passover
is sacrificed,
and in sharing his banquet
we pass with him
from death to life!
He has risen . . .
he is going before us
into his Kingdom!
Alleluia!